W9-BKW-827

WOMEN in the U.S. ARMED FORCES

Women of the U.S. Navy
MAKING WAVES

by Sheila Griffin Llanas

Consultant:
Jessica Williams
Curator of History
Intrepid Sea, Air & Space Museum
New York, New York

CAPSTONE PRESS
a capstone imprint

Snap Books are published by Capstone Press,
151 Good Counsel Drive, P.O. Box 669, Mankato, Minnesota 56002.
www.capstonepub.com

 Books published by Capstone Press are manufactured with paper
containing at least 10 percent post-consumer waste.

Library of Congress Cataloging-in-Publication Data
Llanas, Sheila Griffin, 1958–
  Women of the U.S. Navy : Making Waves / by Sheila Griffin Llanas.
    p. cm. — (Snap. Women in the U.S. armed forces)
  Includes bibliographical references and index.
  ISBN 978-1-4296-5448-7 (library binding)
  1. United States. Navy—Women—Juvenile literature. I. Title. II. Series.

VB324.W65L53 2011
359.0082'0973—dc22   2010040801

Editor: Mari Bolte
Designers: Juliette Peters and Kyle Grenz
Production Specialist: Laura Manthe

Photo Credits:
Alamy: Archive Images, 11, North Wind Picture Archives, 9; Corbis: Bettmann, 15, 16, Sygma/Lee Stone, 17;
Getty Images Inc./Time & Life Pictures/US Navy, 13; NARA , 12; Naval Historical Center Photograph, 10;
U.S. Navy photo, 21, 24, MC1 Chad Runge, 23, MC2 Gregory A. Streit, 5, MC3 James Mitchell, 6, MC3 John
Philip Wagner Jr., 27, MC3 James Mitchell, 7, MCSN Matthew Ebarb, 25, PH2 Michael Sandberg, cover,
PHC Chris Desmond, 19, William Kenny, 26

Artistic Effects:

Shutterstock: Maugli

Printed in the United States of America in North Mankato, Minnesota.
092010   005933CGS11

TABLE of CONTENTS

CHAPTER 1

ABOARD a SUPERCARRIER

Takeoff!

"Jet is on deck," Navy Airman Shaneka McReed said. A Navy jet roared down the flight deck of the aircraft carrier. The jet reached the amazing speed of 160 miles (257 kilometers) per hour in two seconds. Just before it reached the water, Shaneka watched the plane shoot into the air.

Shaneka worked in the primary flight control tower, also known as the "Pry-Fly," aboard the **aircraft carrier** USS *Nimitz*. Her job was to make sure that planes landed and took off safely and on schedule. The sailors in the control tower communicate with the ship's officers and pilots about when aircraft are landing and taking off.

The *Nimitz* is like an airport on the water. Planes use the ship's runway to take off from and land on the **nuclear-powered** supercarrier. The crew of this huge ship can refuel, repair, and store airplanes. The carrier also holds defensive weapons, assists in rescue missions, and polices the seas.

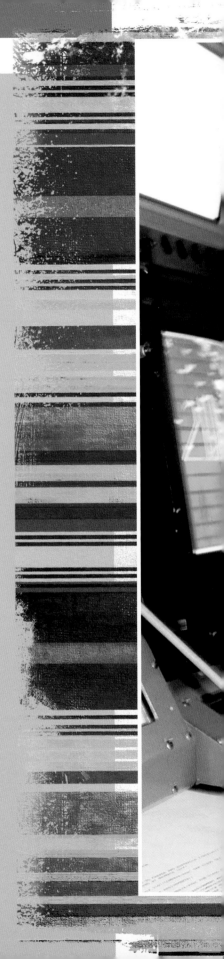

Communication is important aboard huge aircraft carriers like the Nimitz.

aircraft carrier: a warship with a large flat deck where aircraft take off and land

nuclear power: power created by splitting atoms

In 2002 Shaneka graduated from high school in Athens, Georgia. The daughter of a teen mother, Shaneka wanted her life to take a different path.

"I was talking with my grandmother … and told her that I was going to do something with my life," she reflected. Not long after that call, her grandmother passed away. "Well, that's it," Shaneka said. "I've got to start doing something positive for myself." Shaneka joined the U.S. Navy and served two terms aboard the *Nimitz*.

The Nimitz *moved its home port from San Diego, California, to Bremerton, Washington, in 2010.*

A *female sailor directing planes aboard the deck of the* Nimitz

The *Nimitz* is 1,092 feet (333 meters) long and weighs more than 100,000 tons (90,718 metric tons). It carries between 65 and 80 airplanes. The *Nimitz* is like a small town. It has a post office and a hospital. About 19,000 meals are served in the dining hall every day. For six months, the *Nimitz* was Shaneka's home. She sailed all over the world aboard the ship.

The *Nimitz* is home to 4,600 people. Shaneka was one of 400 female sailors aboard. She and the other women played an important role in running the ship. And women are filling an even bigger role in the Navy worldwide. Today women make up more than 15 percent of the U.S. Navy.

CHAPTER 2

A HISTORY of NAVY WOMEN

The U.S. Navy protects the freedom of the nation's seas. With a fleet of almost 300 ships and 4,000 aircraft, the Navy protects U.S. waters during wartime. It also provides rescue and support during natural disasters.

The Navy was formed in 1775. Back then it protected ships from theft and looting by pirates. It also protected the United States during the Revolutionary War (1775–1783). In 1802 the Navy officially barred women from living on ships. However, historians believe female nurses served on ships during that time.

The Navy Nurse Corps

In 1901 the Army formed a Nurse **Corps**. Nursing was a growing field in colleges and universities. More women wanted to serve as nurses in the armed forces. The next year, Navy leaders asked for their own nurse corps, but nothing happened.

corps: a group of military officers and enlisted members

Naval ships helped the United States win the Revolutionary War.

But the Navy needed nurses. New Navy hospitals were being built. Nurses were needed to staff the hospitals. Finally Congress passed the bill on May 13, 1908. The Navy Nurse Corps was born.

Navy nurses had to be single U.S. citizens between the ages of 22 and 44. They were paid fair wages. The first women in the Corps were called the "Sacred Twenty."

the Sacred Twenty, 1908

The Sacred Twenty, and the nurses who followed, worked in Navy hospitals and on ships. They trained local nurses to work with the Navy. They studied advanced medical fields, such as nutrition or physical therapy. They learned to treat wounds during battle.

By 1910, 72 nurses had joined the Navy. Three years later, nearly twice that many were stationed around the country. Nursing was one of the few jobs open to women, and people were beginning to see what Navy women could do. But in a few short years, more nurses would be needed when the United States entered a fierce, bloody war.

Working During World War I

When World War I (1914–1918) broke out in Europe, the United States tried to remain **neutral**. But in 1915, German submarines sank a British ocean liner. The ship was carrying more than 100 American passengers. The United States could no longer stay out of the fight. The Navy was called into duty.

Nearly 1,200 passengers died during the sinking of the ocean liner RMS Lusitania *in 1915.*

neutral: not taking sides

The Navy did not have enough men. But Navy rules did not clearly state that employees must be male. The Navy hired more than 11,000 women for noncombat work in offices and supply rooms. This action freed men to serve overseas.

a group of Yeomen (F), 1918

The new **enlisted** workers were called Yeomen (F). Yeomen were Navy secretaries. F stood for female. Their work and pay were equal to men's. Navy Yeomen (F) did office work, but they also entered technical fields as translators, fingerprint experts, and ship camouflage designers. But when the war ended in 1918, most Navy women were released from duty.

enlist: to join the military

Making WAVES During World War II

More than 20 years later, the United States entered World War II (1939–1945). On December 7, 1941, Japanese airplanes bombed Pearl Harbor in Hawaii. Of the eight battleships in the harbor, four sank and four were damaged. Nearly 2,400 people died, and 1,100 were injured. Navy nurses rushed to treat the wounded.

With the urgency of war, the Navy needed women again. On July 30, 1942, President Franklin D. Roosevelt signed a bill forming the Navy Women's Reserve, also known as Women Accepted for Volunteer Emergency Service (WAVES).

During World War II, Navy women were given more responsibility than ever before.

The Navy's first WAVES enlisted on August 3, 1942. Other women followed. They became the first class of female officers at Smith College in Northampton, Massachusetts. The officer candidates studied military rules, ships and aircraft, and Navy history.

By the end of World War II, there were more than 80,000 women in the WAVES, including 8,000 officers. These women served as flight instructors, cooks, and metalworkers. They worked in communications, **intelligence**, and technology. They were also stationed in Navy hospitals on land. They did jobs women had never done before. But they could not serve in **combat** positions on ships or overseas.

Segregation Ends

In October 1944, the U.S. Navy opened its doors to African-American women. Two months later, Harriet Pickens and Frances Wills became the Navy's first African-American female officers. In June 1948, Congress passed the Women's Armed Services **Integration** Act. The Navy no longer needed to use the name WAVES. Women could now be part of the U.S. Navy, instead of a separate women's reserve.

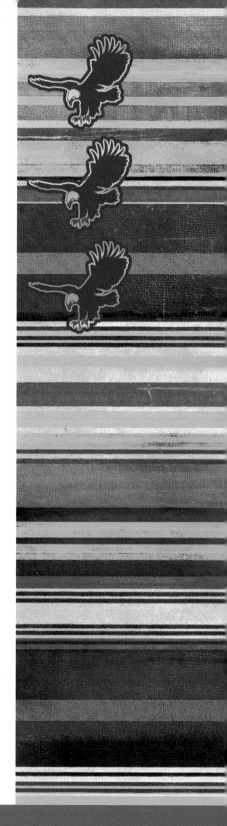

intelligence: secret information about an enemy's plans or actions

combat: fighting between people or armies

The next month, President Harry S. Truman signed a bill that integrated the Navy even more. The bill ended military **segregation** and called for equal treatment of soldiers regardless of their race. At first African-American women made up less than 1 percent of all military women. But today the Navy is much more diverse. The co-ed class of 2013 at the Naval Academy in Annapolis, Maryland, is made up of 35 percent nonwhite students. This is the highest number yet.

Phyllis Mae Daley (third from right) was the Navy's first African-American nurse.

WANTED MORE NAVY NURSES

integration: the practice of including people of all races or genders

segregation: the act of keeping people or groups apart

The 1970s and Beyond

By the 1970s, women had made more Navy firsts. During these years of change, women began asking for more military training.

In 1975 a historic new law allowed women to enroll in military academies. Until the bill passed, only men had attended these schools. The first class of women enrolled the next year. That year the Naval Academy had 81 female students.

In 1978 Congress opened noncombat naval ships to women. The Navy designed separate bunks for women. The first ship to accept women was the USS *Vulcan*.

In 1973 Judith Ann Neuffer became the first woman assigned to flight training in the Navy.

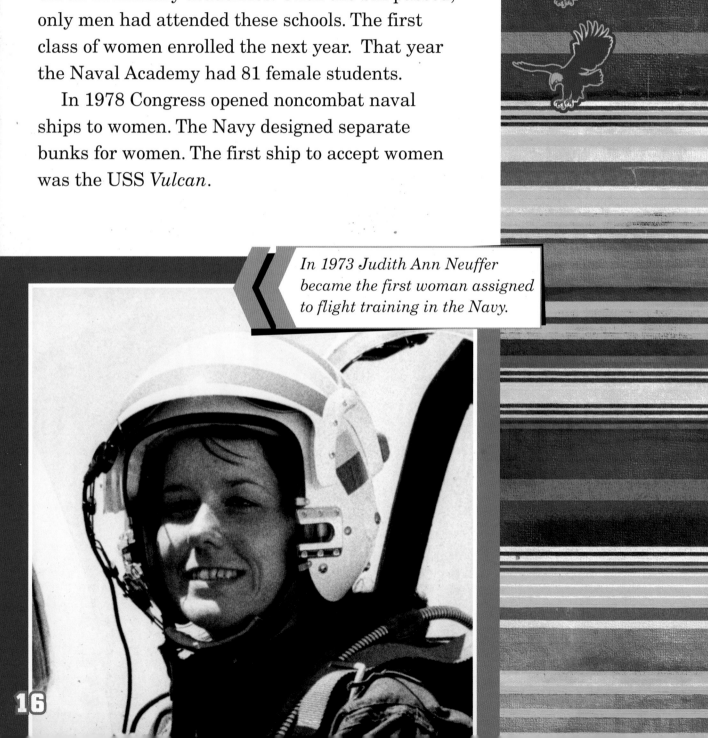

Sailors onboard the USS Eisenhower

Women served on ships during Operation Desert Storm (1991). They continued to show that women could serve just as well as men.

In 1993 Congress allowed women on Navy combat ships. Female officers could finally put their training to use. In 2000 Captain Kathleen McGrath became the first woman to command a U.S. Navy warship. Lieutenant Shannon Workman became the Navy's first female combat pilot.

In 1994 the USS *Eisenhower* became the first ship to have permanent female crewmembers. There were 63 women aboard.

CHAPTER 3

ALL HANDS on DECK

Today the Navy is the nation's second largest military branch. It is divided into nine operating forces. Most forces protect a certain part of the globe. The Navy also carries supplies overseas for the other U.S. military branches. Some sailors are assigned to one of the Navy's 11 active aircraft carriers. Others serve on smaller vessels like destroyers or cruisers.

Boot Camp

All Navy recruits spend eight weeks in basic training, or boot camp. They train at the Great Lakes Naval Training Center near Chicago. The recruits prepare for life at sea. They sleep in dorms called ships. They eat meals in a galley, not a cafeteria. They march and practice weapons exercises inside buildings, as they would on ships. They study first aid and firefighting. They train in swimming, water safety, and survival. They learn ship and aircraft safety.

BATTLE STATIONS

All recruits must pass Battle Stations to become Navy sailors.

In the final weeks of boot camp, Navy recruits must pass a 12-hour test called "Battle Stations." It is a physical and mental test for recruits who will soon be facing the real world.

What would you do during a hurricane? What about during an explosion? What would you do if your teammates were wounded? Every drill and skill learned over the past two months is called into action during Battle Stations.

Officer Training

After basic training, Navy women get assignments. They wear the same uniforms as men. When **deployed**, they serve at least six months on a ship. Working with hundreds of other sailors requires patience and teamwork.

Those who hope to command their own ships train to become officers. There are three ways to become an officer. Sailors can apply to their congressperson for a nomination to the U.S. Naval Academy. They can attend Officer Candidate School after basic training. Or they can go through their college's Naval Reserve Officer Training Corps (ROTC) program.

Widening Horizons at Sea

More Navy women meant more assignments and more historic firsts. The repair ship USS *Samuel Gompers* added to the milestones. In 1979 the *Gompers* became one of the first ships with female crewmembers. In 1992 nearly 30 percent of the crewmembers were women. The average aboard other naval ships was closer to 10 percent. And the *Gompers'* second highest-ranking officer was a woman.

deploy: to position troops for combat

The Navy was the first U.S. military branch to train women as pilots. In 1974 the first women earned their wings. In 1979 Lieutenant Lynn Spruill became the first female pilot qualified to land on aircraft carriers.

As female pilots took to the sky, they filled jobs never before tackled by women. In 1993 Ensign Matice Wright became the Navy's first African-American female flight officer.

Matice Wright has worked for the Naval Academy, the Pentagon, and the White House.

CHAPTER 4

THE NAVY TODAY

WAVES paved the way for the Navy women of today. Because of their hard work, women are now a huge part of the Navy. They serve on ships, as pilots, and in most combat situations. Women cannot participate in ground combat, but can serve in naval and air combat.

Navy Heroes

In 1998 Lieutenant Kendra Williams made history. She became the first American woman to fly a plane on a bombing mission. Stationed aboard the USS *Enterprise*, she piloted a F/A-18 Hornet. She flew the high-tech fighter jet two hours through a pitch-dark night. She scored a hit on an empty military facility over Iraq. Then she flew safely back to her ship.

Many women like Kendra put themselves at risk in the line of duty. Today's Navy women understand the threat of danger. They are trained to react quickly to any situation.

In 2000 Lieutenant Commander Deborah Courtney did not expect disaster. She was serving aboard the USS *Cole* as chief engineer. The *Cole* was refueling near Yemen.

22

A small boat approached the *Cole*. The pilot of the boat looked friendly. He waved to the sailor on watch on the *Cole's* deck. Then he steered his vessel into the side of the *Cole*. The small boat was carrying a bomb that tore a hole in the *Cole's* hull. Seventeen sailors were killed, and another 37 were wounded. The ship's power began to fail. Lights went out throughout the ship. Hallways filled with smoke and black seawater.

No American ship had been sunk by enemy fire since 1945. Deborah would not let her ship be the first. She and the other ship officers began giving orders. The crew got the electricity working and stopped the flooding. Deborah's quick thinking helped save the USS *Cole* from sinking.

Navy women use their skills and discipline on a daily basis. They are trained to leap into action during a crisis. As Navy women rise to the high command, they put their own lives at risk to protect the lives of their crew.

Reaching High Rank

The U.S. Navy's highest rank is admiral. Fewer than 1 percent of Navy officers become admirals. Currently 19 of the Navy's 255 admirals are women. To be eligible to become admirals, officers must serve for at least 20 years. To move up in rank, women make the Navy their lifelong career. They must also be recommended for promotion by higher-ranking officers.

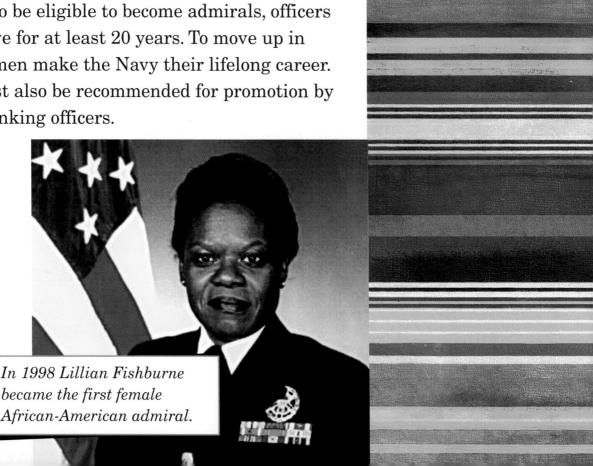

In 1998 Lillian Fishburne became the first female African-American admiral.

The Navy in Numbers

The Navy is smaller today than it was in 1945. During World War II, the number of sailors was at an all-time high with 3.4 million recruits. Today's Navy is much smaller, at only 327,000 in active duty. Ships are more efficient and require smaller crews. But for women, the numbers continue to rise.

In 2000 about 7.5 percent of the Navy was made up of women. By 2008 it was nearly 9 percent. In 2010, 15 percent of the Navy was female. Nearly 8,400 of them were officers. And women make up 20 percent of each graduating class of the United States Naval Academy.

More and more women enter the Naval Academy every year.

Submarines: Women's Last Naval Frontier

As of 2010, women served in 95 percent of all Navy jobs. Navy women had served on combat ships for 16 years. New warships are built for mixed crews of men and women.

Women had been barred from serving on submarines since the first underwater fleet was formed in 1900. Concerns about men and women sharing tight quarters kept women off subs. The ban was finally lifted in April 2010. New subs will be built with separate living quarters for women.

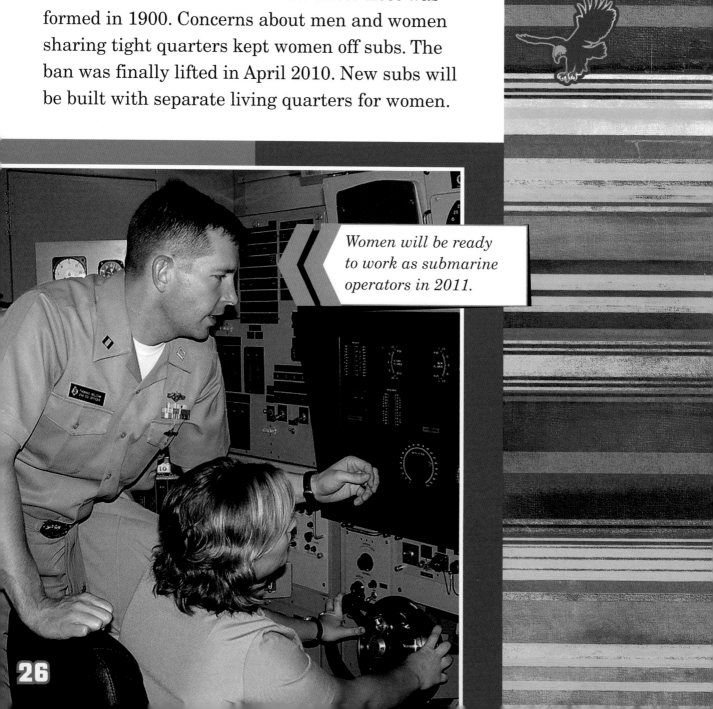

Women will be ready to work as submarine operators in 2011.

"If women can be on space shuttles and on surface ships, I think they ought to be able to work on submarines," said Lisa Goins, a 20-year Navy sailor.

Many Navy men agree. Rear Admiral Sam Locklear was brigade commander at the Naval Academy in 1976. He has seen many changes in the Navy over the years. Recently he said, "I have yet to find a part of our Navy where women can't get the job done as well as men."

It is an exciting time for women in the Navy. There are still more "firsts" for them to accomplish, and more opportunities to explore. Women of the Navy continue to sail into the future.

Navy women continue to explore the skies and seas in order to serve their country.

FAST FACTS

🦅 In 1959 Rear Admiral Grace Murray Hopper invented COBOL, a computer language still used today. The USS *Hopper* is named after her.

🦅 There are 178 Naval ships with women aboard. Of these, 114 ships are run by female officers.

TIMELINE

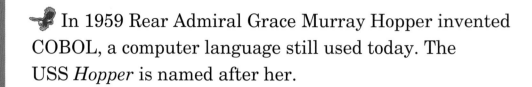

The Navy Reserves is created for women. It is called Women Accepted for Volunteer Emergency Service (WAVES).

The Naval School at Annapolis, Maryland becomes the United States Naval Academy.

Women's Armed Services Integration Act is signed.

1850   **1908**   **1942**   **1944**   **1948**

The Navy Nurse Corps is approved by the Senate. It is the first women's unit in the Navy.

Navy women are allowed to serve overseas in U.S. territories.

🦅 Women can apply for any Navy job except Navy SEALs.

🦅 There have been 14 Navy ships named after women. The most recent was the USNS *Amelia Earhart*.

🦅 Navy ships are at sea 10 to 14 days of every month for training operations. For longer missions, ships deploy every 18 to 24 months.

A law allows women to be promoted to admiral. Until this time, women could be promoted no higher than captain.

Commander Kathleen McGrath is the first American woman to take a warship to sea.

Congress allows women to serve on Navy combat ships.

1967 1993 1994 2000 2010

Navy women serve on a combat ship during wartime.

Congress passes a law allowing Navy women to serve aboard submarines.

GLOSSARY

aircraft carrier (AYR-kraft KAYR-ee-uhr)—a warship with a large flat deck where aircraft take off and land

combat (KOM-bat)—fighting between people or armies

corps (KOR)—a group of military officers and enlisted members

deploy (deh-PLOY)—to position troops for combat

enlist (in-LIST)—to join the military

integration (in-tuh-GRAY-shuhn)—the practice of including people of all races or genders in schools and other public places

intelligence (in-TEL-uh-jenss)—secret information about an enemy's plans or actions

neutral (NOO-truhl)—not taking sides

nuclear power (NOO-klee-ur POU-ur)—power created by splitting atoms; atoms are the smallest part of a substance

segregation (seg-ruh-GAY-shuhn)—the act of keeping people or groups apart

READ MORE

Goldish, Meish. *Navy: Civilian to Sailor.* Becoming a Soldier. New York: Bearport Publishing, 2011.

Hamilton, John. *The Navy.* Defending the Nation. Edina, Minn.: ABDO Pub., 2007.

Jackson, Kay. *Navy Ships in Action.* Amazing Military Vehicles. New York: PowerKids Press, 2009.

INTERNET SITES

FactHound offers a safe, fun way to find Internet sites related to this book. All of the sites on FactHound have been researched by our staff.

Here's all you do:

Visit *www.facthound.com*

Type in this code: 9781429654487

Check out projects, games and lots more at
www.capstonekids.com

INDEX

ABOUT the AUTHOR

Sheila Griffin Llanas has written many Capstone books. She lives in Wisconsin and teaches at the University of Wisconsin-Waukesha and at St. John's Northwestern Military Academy.